FROM A CATERPILLAR TO A BUTTERFLY
(From Birth to Graduation)

Published by Flo's Productions
Website: www.flosproductions.biz
Email: flosproductions@comcast.net or
writersandselfpublishers@yahoo.com
For more information on publishing call: **(810) 394-8612**
Hatchback Publishing Company
(Due to the passing of Florence Dyer)

To have Author Renetta J. Randle speak at your conference, school, retreat, church or to have her for a book signing:

Please contact her at:
SHORTCAKE'S PRODUCTIONS
P.O. Box 13143
Flint, MI 48501-3143
(810) 394-4467
Or Email her at:
SHORTCAKE8PRODUCTIONS@YAHOO.COM

Cover Designed by Fern A. Wilson
Cover Revisions by Flo's Productions

ISBN   0-9789700-0-4
ISBN   978-0-9789700-0-0
Printed in the United States of America

FROM A CATERPILLAR TO A BUTTERFLY
(From Birth to Graduation)

RENETTA J. RANDLE

FLO'S PRODUCTIONS PUBLISHING SERVICE
An Affiliate of Writers & Self Publishers Association

Genesee County

TABLE OF CONTENTS

God Bless...

May God Bless
you in everything.

Seek ye first the Kingdom
of God & his righteousness
+ these things shall be added
unto you.

Love
Lenette

The Joy of the Lord
is your strength
X

Weeping may endure for
a night: but joy cometh
in the morning.
X

ACKNOWLEDGMENTS

To my Lord and Savior Jesus Christ who is the Head of my Life

Mr. and Mrs. Calvin and Pamela Hightower
I love you and thank you for everything!!!

Mr. and Mrs. Robert and Corinne Shackelford
Thank you for just being there when I called no matter what time it was.

Mrs. Mamie Goodson
Thank you for the beginning of my life and teaching me about life.

Bishop Billie K. Bamberg, Pastor Shirley Bamberg and Lady Brittany Bamberg Bishop, thank you all for making me feel apart of your family and for believing in me when I didn't believe in myself, the prophetic words that you spoke into my life, and thank you for being over my life. **YOU ARE** *my Daddy and I love you yesterday, today and forever*
Pastor Shirley, thank you for pushing me forward and keeping me on track, your words will always be in my heart, and thank you for being my Spiritual Mother. I love you.
Lady Brittany, there are no words that can express the way that I feel about you; I love you with all my heart.

Pastor Ronnie and Lady Deborah Wiggins
Thank you for your prayers and believing in me.
Thanks pastor for being the man of God that you are.

I love you both.

Micheline Shackelford, Sydney Mitchell, Calvez Hightower, James White Jr., Lakesha Shackelford, Michelle Shackelford, Robert J.Shackelford, Jr., Leslie Tippins, Earline Brown, Monique Hightower, Toni Hightower and Dyesheika Hightower
My Brothers and Sisters I Love You All

Fern Rayon-Williams and Sheryl Stothers
Thank both of you for all of your love and support that you have given me.

Chandra Walker and Kim McSwain
30 years of friendship means so much and I hope we have 30 more

Darnita Evans, Pamela Lane, Sheneitha Ware, Sabrina Thomas, Sherrod Pigee, Tanisha Sanders, Arlena Honaker, Anton (Lalinda) Honaker, Pauline Duncan, Anoopa Woodward, Nicolia Golden, Joann Lee, Trina (Robert) Hopkins, Charlotte Brown, Roderick LeGardye, Charity Billings, Gerald Traeye, Robin Scales, Virginia Billups, Tonika Moye, Charles, Steffon and Sheldon Smith, LeShelle Johnson, Dr. Larry Young and Dr. Shawn Wiggins, Jackie Thompson
I thank each one of you. In some way, you have touched my life in a very special way; I love you all very much.

For those that were not mentioned please forgive me and thank you too.

DEDICATIONS

*This book is dedicated to my two wonderful children
and my beautiful daughter in-law, Mr. Cory (Ardrika)
Banks and Ms. Stephani Randle
Always trust in and believe in God. Believe in yourself
and always follow your dreams.
I love you all so much!!*

*To my six beautiful grandchildren, Arriyana, Ja'Kyra,
Corionte, Corion, Samyria and Arrielle
God bless all of you.
Granny loves you with all my heart.*

*To every man, woman, boy or girl that will or has
overcome that giant obstacle that will change your life
forever.*

IN LOVING MEMORY

Grandma Barbara Jean Phillips
March 24, 1927 - October 4, 1989
Grandma...I miss so many things about you. You were
the most beautiful lady that I have ever known. I wish
that you could see all of the children that are a part of
you, I love you so much

Aunt Leslie Jean Sanders
December 13, 1943 – June 5, 1984
Thank you for loving me like a daughter I love and miss
you so much

Lavette Jones
July 19, 1958 – December 24, 1996
My dear friend I enjoyed every moment that we spent
together and every talk that we had, you were my
sister....and I miss you so much

Mr. Michael Wendell Johnson, Jr.
(JR)
October 28, 1978 – December 22, 1996
I love and miss you very much

FROM THE PUBLISHER

Instantly, after meeting with Author Renetta Randle, I knew I'd been divinely setup. Ms. Randle has a very free, open spirit and very eager to learn. Publishing *From a Caterpillar to a Butterfly* has been an honor for me. I really feel that readers are going to be truly blessed through Ms. Randle's story. She is a remarkable lady and truly exposes the enemy and all his evil devices. Through publishing *From a Caterpillar to a Butterfly* I've learned there is nothing we can't overcome. I believe Ms. Randle is here for such a time as this as a voice for victims of sexual abuse. I salute her for the courageous spirit she has for sharing *From a Caterpillar to a Butterfly* with the world. Author Renetta Randle thank you for allowing Flo's Productions to handle all your publishing needs. I wish you the best with all your future endeavors.

Sincerely,
Florence Dyer
Author/Publisher/Graphic Designer
CEO of Flo's Production

FOREWARD

Pretty dresses, nice shoes, pony tails with cute ribbons, barbie dolls, the first day of kindergarten, meeting and spending time with friends, the first day of Junior High School, a first boyfriend, 9th grade prom, the first Day of High School, the high school prom and Graduation. All of these events are a representation of wonderful memories a young girl should have for the rest of her life, but somewhere along the way something or someone could change your destiny.

My life wasn't quite like that; how about abandonment, kidnapping, incest, teenage pregnancy and promiscuity all by age 18. Covering up was something that I could do very well; it became so common that I believed that everything was great in my life.

Before the metamorphosis of a butterfly can be completed, the caterpillar has to mature from the egg to the larva. Just as in my life, I had to mature from a wounded young girl to a healed woman that was ready to begin a new life. There were so many things I had to endure to get to that butterfly.

II Corinthians 4:17 states "For our light affliction, which is but for a moment, is working for us a far more exceeding and eternal weight of Glory."

1.
BORN

My mother was fifteen, wild and in love with my dad. She would do any and everything she could to see him. She told me that she tried to run away from home just to see him because her parents wouldn't allow her to see him the way that she wanted. She lived with her Godparents who were very strict on her. This was a good, Christian family and my mother was not the good, Christian girl they wanted her to be. She defied everything that they would tell her to do. So, when she found out that she was pregnant, it made things even worse. She was told by her godmother that she couldn't live with them anymore and that she was a disgrace to this Christian family. There was nothing else that she could do but to tell my daddy that she had no where to live. She couldn't go back and live with her mother, because of the abuse that her mother had endured and she didn't make things good for herself when she lived there. She had witnessed her mother being abused by her stepfather over and over again. So she vowed that she would not go back to that environment.

I remember seeing pictures of my mother when she was a young girl, she was this short, chunky girl with long, coal black hair; her skin looked so smooth and she was very pretty. She reminded me of a little Indian girl. In those pictures she appeared so innocent, but to know her; she was a big rebel.

Daddy was seventeen and he lived with his mother and three younger brothers. He knew that he had to tell my grandmother that my mother was pregnant. Now my grandmother did not like my mother, because she thought that my mother was too wild for him. My grandmother was not about to let her ruin his life, but my daddy loved my mother and insisted that my mother stay with them. My grandmother agreed, but only on one condition, that my mother and father were to get married.

My daddy left his house to get my mother and tell her the good news; he wanted to marry her and they could live with his mother. My mother told me she was not very happy about having to live with my grandmother, but she loved my dad, so she did it.

After they were married, they moved in with my grandmother and my three uncles. My grandmother made space for them, downstairs in the livingroom and everyone else slept upstairs.

It was time for me to make my appearance; my mother was rushed to the hospital, after being in labor for 13 hours. I was born at 10:58pm on August 25, 1961 at Buttersworth Hospital in Grand Rapids, MI.

My mother named me Renetta Jeanette Shackelford. She named me this because she didn't want me to be named me after my father (literally after him). He wanted me to be named Roberta, and she was not about to name me that, because she thought that was a name for an old lady. She told me how she came to name me Renetta.

She was sitting around the house trying to come up with a name that would be suitable for me. She said that she wanted me to have the same initials as my dad's; and she had to have a name that was very unique. When my dad got home later that day, she sat down with him and told him about the name and he agreed.

My middle name is very special to my family, it came from my maternal grandmother and my mother's oldest sister, and both of their middle names were Jean. Being my mother's first girl, she wanted my middle name to be Jean, but she said that Renetta Jean didn't sound right so she had to add something to it to it sound better, so she decided on Jeanette.

After my mother and I were released from the hospital, she and my dad took me to live with them in my grandmother's house. When I was about three months old, they began to fight almost every night; this went on until I was six months old. Mama told me that one night they had gotten in the biggest fight ever.

This fight was so bad that my mother waited until my dad went to sleep, boiled a pot of water, poured cream of wheat into it and threw them on him. Daddy jumped up running and screaming so loud that it woke up my grandmother; she came downstairs to find out what happened and of course she took my daddy's side. This made my mother very angry; she told both of them that she was tired of the abuse and she was leaving.

After everything had calmed down and everyone had gone to bed, my mother packed her bags and left; leaving me with my daddy and grandmother.

2.
LEFT BEHIND

Daddy had no idea how to take care of a baby, so he asked my grandmother to help him. After about two months of taking care of me, he was drafted into the military. He knew that he had to tell my grandmother and she would probably be upset with him. My mother had already abandoned me and now my father was forced to do the same, what else could she do; him well and kept me.

I called her mama, because she was the only mother that I knew. She took very good care of me and she was raising me as her own daughter. She spent a lot of time teaching me how to read and write my name by buy me a typewriter. After I learned how to spell my name using the typewriter, she bragged to everyone about the way that I learned.

On my second birthday, my daddy came home to see me. I only knew him from the picture that my grandmother had of him in an army uniform that sat on top of the television in her living room.

When he arrived he was wearing a green army uniform with lots of strips and medals. He looked just like the picture I saw. He was short, and his skin was a caramel color. He had a short hair cut and I remembered that he had a mustache because it was very thick.

He walked into the house and spoke to everyone. He then asked me to come over and give him a hug. He sat me on his lap and began to talk to me; he called me by the name of Rae. He asked me questions about my stay with my grandmother. We talked for a little while longer and then he asked me if I'd like to get some ice cream.

When we got into the car he told me that he wanted me to come and live with him, but I had to wait until he got settled.

When we got to the ice cream parlor, I ordered a vanilla ice cream cone; my favorite. I was so excited to just be there with my dad that I would have eaten any flavor. We sat outside and ate our ice cream together and talked until it was almost dark.

When we got back to my grandmother's house, he walked over to where she was sitting and hugged her, and told everyone goodbye. He then came over to where I was and told me that he would see me later, but until then I was to continue to do as my grandmother says. That was the last that I saw of my daddy for a very long time.

I'm sure after a couple of days I had forgotten everything that my daddy said to me. As long as I had the love of my grandmother and my uncles, nothing else mattered.

3.

MEETINGS

I must have been about three years old when I met my cousin Norm; he was my Uncle's son. His mother would bring him over to my grandmother's house everyday before she went to work. Norm was the second grandchild on my dad's side and we played together like brother and sister.

Norm was this funny looking little boy, with a smile that would melt your heart. He was only about one and a half year's old, bow-legged and he reminded me of a little baby monkey; but he was my cousin and I loved him very much.

I really don't think my grandmother would have known how to function without us. She would take us everywhere she went, because we were her babies. .

When I was about four years old, I remember going into the kitchen to get something to drink, I noticed some little brown or black bugs crawling all around. I started screaming and asking her what they were and why were there so many of them. They must have been there all along and I was just too young to remember seeing them.

My grandmother was sitting in the living room with Norm, when she told me they were roaches and told me to calm down, but I continued to scream. She came into the kitchen to show me that they wouldn't hurt me by stomping her feet, this made them run away. I still wanted to know why it was so many of them, but she would not answer me, instead she took me back into the living room and told me to sit on the couch next to Norm and nothing else was said about it.

My maternal grandmother would come to visit me quite often, and when she came she had a little girl with her. This little girl was a few years younger than me, but we got along really good. After we played together for a couple of weeks, they decided to sit us down and tell us that we were sisters.

There was no way that we would have thought that we were sisters because we didn't look anything alike. Her skin was very dark and her hair was very short and my skin was very light almost white. I had very long hair, but it did not make any difference to us what our skin color was, we just wanted to be together.

Whenever it was time for her to leave we would cry, because we thought we were not going to see each other again, but our grandmothers' made sure that we played together almost everyday.

I would ask my sister did she ever see our mother, because I could only remember her coming to visit a few times. My sister was only two years old, so she really didn't understand anything about my mother, because our maternal grandmother was the only mother that she knew. I really didn't know the relationship that my mother and her mother had, but I wanted it to be better then what my mother and paternal grandmother had.

My mother would only come and visit me every six to eight months and it remained that way until my mother decided that she wanted me back. She started to visit more often and began to tell me that she was coming back to get me. She didn't want me to tell my grandmother because she knew that if she found out that my grandmother would stop her from coming to see me. My mother didn't understand that I loved my grandmother, and I told her what my mother said.

My grandmother told me that my mother was lying, and that she was only saying that to make me feel better because she had left me in the first place. My grandmother loved me so much and didn't want to see me go and she didn't want to see me get hurt.

She said my mother wanted to live her own life without having to take care of children and that I would only be in her way. So she told me that I shouldn't believe anything she was saying, and she wasn't really coming to take me away from her and we were not to talk about it ever again.

4.

KIDNAPPED

I had just turned five years old and it was time for me to go to school. My grandmother enrolled me in kindergarten at Jefferson Elementary School, in Grand Rapids, MI. On the first day of school during recess, my mother came to see me. She reminded me that she was still coming to get me so that I could live with her; she told me that she loved me and left.

When my grandmother picked me up from school, I told her that my mother had come to see me that day and told me again that she would be coming to get me. My mother knew that there was no way that my grandmother would allow her to just take me, and that the school was not going to allow that to happen either.

I finished out the rest of the week at Jefferson and that Saturday afternoon I was playing on the porch and my grandmother was sitting in the window watching me as she always did. The phone started ringing and she told me not to move while she answered it.

From out of no where, my mother ran up to me and pulled me off the porch. She pushed me into a car where there was a man sitting in the driver's seat ready to drive off. I was screaming for my grandmother and as I turned around in the car I could see her running down the street after the car.

After I calmed down, I noticed my sister Cheli was also in the car. My mother had taken her from my other grandmother's house just as she had taken me. There was also little boy in the car with us, I asked my mother who he was she stated that this was my brother, JaJa.

My mother had been married, divorced and had another child I began to cry again and asked her if I was going back to see my grandmother. She said she would take me back after we were settled in our new place.

What a new place we went to; it was my mother's boyfriend's, sister's house in Flint, MI. Aunt Sallie, she had six children; Ricky, Vett, Laura, Kurt, Matt and Faith. They all lived in a 3 bedroom house. They were introduced as my cousins, this meant that there would be two more adults and three more kids living in this house, and we did it for about a year.

When we moved in with them I was still only five years old and my mother enrolled me in the school down the street. It had the same exact name of the school that I was going to in Grand Rapids, Jefferson Elementary School.

I loved this school and my new teacher; she was very nice and attentive to all of her students. She also took out special time to help me learn how to read a lot better than I had already learned while I was living with my grandmother.

One day after I had gotten out of school, I came home and my mother wasn't there, I began to cry because my mother was always there. My mother had gotten really sick and had to be rushed to the hospital, she had to stay for about three days, but it seemed like a lifetime.

While she was in the hospital, I was left at home with my Aunt's kids, my sister and brother. Aunt Sallie wasn't home often because she worked a lot. She reminded me of Popeye's girlfriend, Olive Oil; very tall and thin. She worked in the shop (General Motors) and she worked second shift so we were left at home with Cousin Ricky. My mom's boyfriend stayed at the hospital with her.

That night, I was supposed to have been asleep upstairs along with the other kids, but I noticed that my cousins Vett and Laura were not upstairs and I wanted to know where they were. So, I got out of the bed and went downstairs to look for them. I could hear my cousin Ricky because he was talking so loud.

I went to see where I heard the voices coming from, they were coming from in the bathroom, but I couldn't hear what they were talking about until I walked up closer to the door. I heard Vett and Laura crying, so I opened up the bathroom door to ask why they were crying and saw two older boys having sex with my cousins.

These were young girls, only five and seven years old, and from what I could see, they did not want any part of what was going on. After my cousin noticed I was standing there, he tried to make me come in the bathroom and have sex with the same two boys. I don't remember if I said no or not but I ran back upstairs and jumped in the bed. He came running after me telling me that he was going to beat my butt if I didn't get back downstairs. I told him that I was going to tell my mother when she got out of the hospital. He threatened me saying that if I told on him, that every time my mother leaves he was going to tie me to the bed and beat the **HELL** out of me.

Now Ricky was about 15 years old and he was much bigger than all the other kids. He was the one that was always left in charge when the grown ups were gone and the majority of the time we were left with this fool. He was the kind of person, that if he told one of us to do something we had better do it or pay the consequences when the adults were gone; which meant we would get a beating.

He got a belt and came upstairs to whip me. Right before he hit me, my mother and her boyfriend walked in. She must have heard me crying because she came upstairs. My mother asked me why was I crying, I started telling her what had happened, but by the time I got finished telling her he had cleared out the house and convinced them that I wouldn't do what I was told and somehow convinced my cousins not to tell.

5.

BEATINGS

From that point on, my cousin continued to fight me on a daily basis. Whenever my mother was gone he would get a belt and spank me for any and everything. There was one particular time my mother went on an overnight trip and left us with him. So as soon as they left, my cousin made me go upstairs and lay across the bed face down.

He tied my hands and feet to each side of the bed, I asked him what was he going to do and his exact words to me were I told you that I was going to beat the **HELL** out of you and that is what I am going to do. After I was completely tied down, he went and got a belt and beat me, no matter how hard I screamed he would continue hitting me and he did this until he got tired. When he was done beating me he left me tied to the bed all night long.

The next morning he came into the room to see if I was awake, he came over to the bed and saw that there was wet spot. He started screaming at me, telling me that I should have told him that I had to go to the bathroom. He walked out the room and when he came back he had the same belt and started beating me again. I was screaming so loud that he didn't hear my mother come upstairs and walk into the room.

My mother started screaming and hitting him, and made him untie me. She told him that there is nothing that anyone could have done to deserve this. He tried to explain to my mother why he did what he did, but she would not listen to him. I told her why he was doing this to me and how long that it had been going on.

She went downstairs and got her boyfriend (his uncle) and told him that she found him beating me and that I was tied up. My mother's boyfriend went upstairs, tied him to the bed, beat him just as he had beat me. I could hear him screaming just as I was screaming, I heard my mother's boyfriend tell him that as long as he lived he better not ever touch me again.

That incident made my mother very angry to the point that she found her own place to live. She packed up her three kids, all of her belongings and moved into a two-room apartment.

6.

MOVED

We moved into to our new apartment even though it was only two rooms; a living room and one bedroom. We loved it. I was so happy just to have my own bed to sleep in. My mother bought us a set of bunk beds. I slept on the top and my sister slept on the bottom. My brother was still young so he slept in the living room with my mother and her boyfriend.

After we got settled in, I met my first friend, Tammy. She lived across the street with her grandmother, mother and brother. We played together everyday and became best friends.

Tammy had the strangest relationship with her mother. She and her brother called their mother by her first name and that was perfectly okay with her. Now at the time, it seemed pretty cool, until I tried it on my mother, I walked into the house and called my mother Pam. I told her that Tammy called her mother by her first name and she didn't get into any trouble and that was all that I remembered saying, because I got slapped so hard that I could see stars and almost lost my two front teeth.

I learned a valuable lesson that day that will stay with me for the rest of my life. **DO NOT CALL YOU MOTHER BY HER FIRST NAME WITHOUT PERMISSION!!!**

7.
WALKER

I was in the first grade and it was time for me to go to my new school. This school was about 8 blocks away and my family did not have a car; so that meant that I walked to school everyday, rain, sleet, hail, or snow.

I had gotten up late one morning, which meant that I had to walk to school by myself. I walked though a grassy field because the neighbors could see those kids that had to walk by themselves. I had on some black dress shoes, a checkered red and black skirt and a white shirt, and all I remember was that I was running as fast as I could. I was being chased by some dogs and I ran right out of my shoes and I didn't stop running until I got to school.

When I got to my class, my teacher asked me what had happened, because I didn't have on any shoes. I told her that some dogs chased me and I left them in the field. She called and told my mother what had happened and that I had left my shoes. My mother asked if I was okay and if so that I had better go and find my shoes as soon as I got out of school because she had just purchased them.

That day I walked around without shoes and as soon as school was out I went back to look for my shoes. Sure enough my shoes were exactly where I had left them; I put them on and went home.

Later during the school year, I had the pleasure of meeting a young lady by the name of Sheila. She was very nice. Sheila was a quiet girl and some of the kids took advantage of that. We became good friends and started walking to and from school together.

One day while we were walking to school some of the kids started punching and shoving her around, they continued to do this all the way to school. When we arrived at school she was crying and telling them to leave her alone. When we got to our class, she was still crying. Before she could say anything, the other kids told the teacher that I was picking on her.

My teacher came over to my desk and asked me what had happened and I told her, then she asked my friend what happened and she wouldn't tell her, because she was scared that the other kids would beat her up on the way home. They convinced my teacher that it was me so she sent me to the principal's office.

Now this was one of the meanest principals that I could ever remember having. She didn't even ask me what had happened. She got out the paddle (yes, at that time your parents didn't have to be called for permission, everything was left to the principal's discretion). She told me to bend over and touch my toes and I got a big swat. At that time, if an authority figure wanted to chastise you they could and you better not even think about talking back. After that swat, I began crying and trying to explain that it was not me that was picking on her, but she still wouldn't listen.

Later that day, my friend walked up to the teacher and told her what happened, my teacher called the Principal down and told her what she had just been told. The Principal walked out and went back down to her office. She instructed my teacher to send me down to her office. She began to apologize to me, but that didn't take away the fact that I was telling the truth from the very beginning.

When I got home from school, I told my mother what happened. She was so angry about the whole situation, that I saw tears in her eyes. The next morning instead of going to work, she went up to the school with me and talked to the Principal. From that day forth my mother made sure that anytime someone blamed something on me, whether I did it or not, it was thoroughly investigated before anything was done.

The next year was totally different, I became more aggressive. My attitude completely changed toward my schoolmates. I remember having a friend, or at least she thought that we were friends, in my gym class. This girl was very timid and I took advantage of her. Everyday for the about a year I constantly picked on her. I would pick on her on the way to school and also on the way home. Until one day she decided to tell her older sister what was going on.

After school one day, her sister came to pick her up and walk her home. All I remember was hearing her sister say to her, "you better fight her back." Well, this day I didn't even think about bothering her and the next thing I remember was we were fighting, and she was kicking my butt. What I didn't realize was her sister told her that if she didn't whip me, she had to fight her and she didn't want to fight her sister because she was twice our size. After that fight, I did not bother her or anybody else for that matter and we really did become friends.

Third grade was the year I had to prove myself. There was this bully that lived down the street from me and everybody was afraid of her. She would make all the kids fight each other and if we didn't she would beat us up.

I was outside playing one afternoon and she came down the street and started picking on me. I ran inside and told my mother that this girl was outside bothering me. My mother told me that if I didn't go outside and fight this girl that I would have to fight my mother. She opened up the front door, pushed me outside and locked the door behind her.

When everything was all over, my mother was came outside to see what happened. She found that I had won the fight and I didn't have any more trouble with this girl and neither did anyone else on the block. I guess that I was so afraid of my mother that I had a better chance of winning outside than winning inside.

During Christmas that year, I found out some bad news. I woke up at about 2am to go to the bathroom and I heard some noise in the living room; I got excited because I thought that I was going to see Santa Claus putting our toys under the Christmas tree. Instead I saw my mother and her boyfriend putting toys under the tree. I asked my mother where was Santa Claus, she apologized and told me that she was the only Santa Claus.

Being only eight years old, this really devastated me for a very long time because my mother had always taught us that there was a Santa Claus and to find out like that there wasn't it hurt.

I told my mother that when I grow up and have children that I wouldn't let them believe that there was a Santa Claus, because I didn't want them to feel the hurt I was feeling. My mother hugged me, apologized again for me being hurt, walked me back to my room, told me to get back to bed and go back to sleep.

After the New Year, I overheard my mother and some of the neighbors discussing that some of the families will have to move because of a new highway construction taking place. My mother and her boyfriend were talking to some men about us getting a new house but we didn't no how long it would be before we would get it.

It was about two weeks before the end of third grade and we moved into our new house that the city had built for us. This house was very nice, it was a tri-level home with three bedrooms, a bath and a half with all appliances and a fenced-in yard. Across the street was a park where everyone in the neighborhood played. It had a swing set, a slide and the best thing about it was the baseball field.

My mother enrolled us in Carpenter Road Elementary School located down the street. The first day of school, was almost the last day of the school, but I met a lot of new kids to spend the summer with.

That summer was wonderful, I got to know more kids in the neighborhood and we all played at the park everyday.

Fourth grade was the grade to remember for the rest of my life. The beginning of it was wonderful; I had a very loving and caring teacher. Mrs. Brown, she was the best teacher that I ever had. She was my homeroom, art and math teacher, she also was the teacher that showed me how to act like a young lady.

She asked each student to create a picture of anything we wanted; I started drawing lines everywhere on my paper. It must have been something that no one else had ever done; because this drawing won first place at an art show that she took me to.

Mrs. Brown cared about us so much that she invited a few of the students to come over and ride snowmobiles. Her husband even took the time out to show each one of us how to steer the snowmobiles.

Mrs. Brown, being the loving person that she was tried to protect me from one of my classmates; this girl would fight me everyday just for coming to school, she would just see me and start a fight with me.

At the end of the fourth grade, we got into a big fight and I won so she decided that she was going to get her sister to fight me after school. I told my teacher what was going on, because I was really tired of fighting this girl; and now I had to fight someone else in her family, yeah right. So, Mrs. Brown kept me inside her classroom until she thought everything had died down. She told me that it was safe for me to go home and as I was walking to my house, she was waiting for me and we began to fight again.

When the fight was over she ran home and came back with her sister. I thought that I was going to have to fight her sister, but she didn't want to be involved so that was the end of us fighting.

9.

MOLESTED

I was nine years old, asleep in my bed, and was awakened by a hand inside of my pajamas fondling me. This startled me so much I started to cry and kept my eyes closed because I was so scared. I didn't know what to think, the only thing that went through my head was it was a monster.

When I opened my eyes, I realized that it was my stepfather doing this to me. I asked him what he was doing and why was he doing this. He said that this happens to all little girls my age, but I couldn't tell anyone, because it was our little secret and if I kept this secret that he would buy me anything that I wanted, so I kept quiet.

I guess this night was his preparation night, because the only thing that he did was touch me and ask me if this felt good. I told him that I didn't like it and he told me that eventually that I would, then he left and when back downstairs.

My stepfather worked third shift, so that mean he was not home at night during the week, but he would always be home on the weekends. So during the day while we were getting ready for school, he would be there staring at me. I made it very clear to him that I did not want these advances, but he would not stop.

My mother always went to bed early during the week and on the weekend she would always stay downstairs watching television with my stepfather until she fell asleep. He would sneak upstairs into my bedroom, and he would stand by my bed. He would whisper in my ear to let me know that he was there, he then proceeded to pull my pajamas bottoms down, while telling me to be quiet.

He spread my legs apart and he would put his finger inside my vagina. While he had his finger inside of me he would be moving then in and out, he would be moaning and asking me how it felt. I was always too scared to say anything so I would just cry.

He stayed in my room for a long time and continued doing this over and over again to me. One night after he had left out of my room, I ran downstairs to find my mother, she was in the kitchen and I was crying. I told her what he had done to me, she walked me into the living room and asked him was this true. He convinced my mother that I must have been dreaming so she made me go back upstairs and go to sleep. I felt so betrayed by my mother, this man was raping her daughter and all she could say to me was go back to sleep.

For about three weeks he didn't bother me, and everything had calmed down and nothing else was said about it, started all over again. He continued this kind of sexual act every weekend until I turned about 11 years old, and then he must have decided that I was old enough to actually have intercourse with him.

The weekend before the worst started happening to me, my mother wanted our bunk beds taken down. She felt as though we were too old to have the beds bunk anymore. Why did she do that? It only gave him more room to do what he wanted to me.

The first time it happened after the beds were taken down, he came into my room and sat on the floor while I was asleep. He covered my mouth and whispered in my ear not to make any noise, he pulled my pajama bottoms down, spread my legs apart and began penetrating me first with his fingers, and this time I could feel that he was using more than one finger.

I remember him saying to me that you are very wet down there, I had no idea what he meant at that time and I was not going to ask him and he told me to scoot over and he got in my bed.

He pulled down his underwear and started penetrating me again with his fingers, he then pushed my legs even farther apart, he got in between them steady push them apart and he began to penetrate me with his penis. I started crying and he covered my mouth so that no one could hear me. I told him that it hurt and I wanted him to stop, but he told me that it would only hurt for a minute and that it should start to feel good. He continued to push himself inside of me stopping for a few seconds and then he would continue to push until he couldn't push against me any more.

His body was so heavy on mine that every time he would move it felt as though I was being smothered. He did not care. If I tried to say anything at all regarding this he would tell me to be quiet or just cover my mouth again.

When he was done, he got up, he went into the bathroom and then went back downstairs as usual. I stayed in my bed crying until I felt safe enough to go to the bathroom. When I entered the bathroom, I remember seeing blood, I did understand why there was blood, but I couldn't tell my mother because she didn't believe me the first time that I tried to tell her.

I cleaned myself up, went and got back in my bed and cried myself to sleep. I knew that he was not coming back that night because I could hear my mother walking around. I didn't understand why he was doing this, but I knew it wasn't right.

I remember getting sick and having to stay home from school. I was asleep in my bedroom and was awakened by my naked stepfather, standing in front of me trying to ease my panties down. I told him that I didn't want him to do this to me anymore and I tried to pull my panties back up, he was much stronger than me.

He just pushed my legs apart with his leg as he was getting on top of me, penetrating me with his fingers. Once he was all the way on top of me and began pushing himself inside of me over and over again this seemed like it went on for hours.

When he got up he told me that I had better not tell my mother or she would be mad and that he would kill both of us. I had gotten to the place that I became immune to him coming in my room. I just wanted it to be over when he came to get me. So when he did come I wouldn't even fight anymore, because what was the use. Nobody knew what was going on and I didn't want anything to happen to my mother.

I started stayed away from home as much as I could and every weekend I would literally ask my friends to ask their parents if I could spend the night, but I never told a soul what was happening to me. The nights that I couldn't stay with friends, I would sleep with my covers wrapped around me, but that didn't matter he would just unwrap them, do what he wanted to do and leave.

To make matters even worse, my mother didn't get home until late on most days, so that meant that I was home after school. I hated walking by this man because he would make sexual gestures toward me, like stick his tongue out at me, touch me inappropriately and he would even show me his private parts.

During the summer, before going to the seventh grade, I began to develop breasts and began getting my pubic hair. This is a sacred time in any young girl's life, a very private moment, but not for me.

I had just started Junior High School and I was well developed, I remember this day my mother had already left for work, and my sibling was downstairs eating breakfast.

I got out of my bed and I went into the bathroom to take a bath, I started running the water and started to take my pajamas off when he came into the bathroom and locked the door behind him. He started fondling my breast and saying to me you are starting to become a woman, than he looked down at my private area and saw that I was getting my pubic hair and began to touch me.

I told him to get out and he said he would eventually, so he made me just stand there while he slowly fondled every part of my body and told me that before any boy saw me like this or touched me he was going be the first to have me like this. He made me lay down on the floor; he laid on top of me and started kissing me in my mouth and on my breast. Then, he started pushing my legs apart and inserted his fingers inside my vagina, he made that same statement again about me being wet enough and started penetrating me with his penis on the bathroom floor of our house with my sibling downstairs.

Now I was old enough to understand why he would put his fingers inside of me before he inserted his penis. This is the way he stimulated me before he raped me. He got up and told me not to move. I was too terrified to do any thing else so I just laid there scared because I didn't want him to hurt my siblings.

He left out of the bathroom and I could hear him go downstairs and tell my brother and sister to get ready to go to school, I heard my sister ask where I was and he told her that I was taking a bath. I could also hear him trying hurry up and get them out of the house.

When they were gone, he came back upstairs to tell me that I would not be going to school that day. He had told my siblings that I was sick and that is what I was going to tell my mother when she got home from work. He made me go and get in my bed and said to me that he was going to make sure that I was going to be very well broken in when I get a boyfriend, He continued to rape me until it was time for my siblings to come home.

From that day on he didn't rape me anymore, but the gestures continued. It seemed as though I was finally free, and believe me I didn't even want to think about any part of that horrible period in my life. But the monster was already created, I had bottled up so much hatred toward my mother for not believing me and toward my stepfather for taking away my innocence that I began to fill my life with friends, but I was very angry.

The Junior High School that I attended was majority Caucasian. They tried very hard to intimidate some of the black students and because of what I had already been through in my life, I was not about to be their little punching bag or even someone that they could insult every time they wanted to, so I decided that if they even tried to intimidate me that I was going to fight back.

Through all the abuse that I had experienced, there was a special young man that I was very much attracted to. He was tall, dark and handsome. I don't think that he even knew I existed, but it must have been something because I got into a fight with a girl about him. The bad part about the whole situation was that neither of us were his girlfriend. A group of us kids were getting ready to walk home, when this girl started following and threatening me. She told me that she had liked him for over a year and that I was not about to come and take him. I told her that this guy was not thinking about me, but if she just wanted to fight, I was not going to let her beat me. There was no way that I was going to fight over a boy, but if she hit me I would fight her and she hit me. Well the fight was on, I really don't know who won that fight, and I didn't care. I just wanted her to know that she could not get away with that.

Later on in the school year, I was standing at my locker between classes when two white girls decided that they were going to start picking on me by bumping into me and laughing. I hit one of them back and we started fighting. I got kicked out because they told the principal that I started the fight and he believed them.

The principal called my mother and told her that I was kicked out and that she had to come and get me. When she got there she was very angry. At first I thought that she was mad at me, but after she finished talking to the principal she told me that she was tired of this school and that I would be transferred to the school next door to where she worked.

I finished up the rest of the year at Lowell and just like my mother said she transferred me to the school next door to where she worked. The name of this school was Emerson Jr. High; it was a great experience for me. It took me to another level, I was in the eighth grade and I didn't know anyone there, but everyone seemed to be very nice. I got along with just about everyone I met that year. There were two girls that I immediately become friends with; they treated me like we had known each other all of our lives.

Now there is always that one girl that hated everybody, and of course I was no exception. I was the new girl on the block and a lot of the boys would talk to me. That was reason enough for her not to like me, but she never said anything to me that year.

As I became more acquainted with everyone, I met my first boyfriend Lonnie. He was in the ninth grade, tall, handsome, very popular, and he had an identical twin brother.

Lonnie was very sweet, but he always stayed in trouble. I really grew to like him very much, but just as we started to become close, my phone at home got turned off and there was no way for me to communicate with him except at school and this caused a problem for us.

He finally got into enough trouble that he got expelled for just about the remainder of the school year. He was sent to a boot camp (detention center). I missed him very much.

His twin brother was still there, he reminded me so much of him. I was walking in the hall one day when he stopped me and pulled me into a doorway. We started kissing, I just wanted it to be Lonnie so bad that I continued to kiss his brother not knowing that someone saw us and told his girlfriend. Some kind of way they got a message to Lonnie and that was the end of our relationship.

I had no intentions of this happening and I wasn't sure if he did either. We talked afterwards and he told me that every time that he talked to his brother all he talked about was me and that he knew that I missed him very much, so he said he was a little jealous and that was the reason why he kissed me.

About a month later, I started dating another ninth grader; this was about the time when my mother let me attend our school dances. I was hanging out with some girls that were older than me. The twins as everyone called them, they were very pretty, short and dark skinned and all the guys like them. My mother thought that since they lived behind us it would be ok.

They came over and asked my mother if could I go to the dance with them and she allowed me to go. The only thing that I learned from going to the dances was hanging out on the wall hugged up with boys. So to be a part of the crowd; that is exactly what I did with my boyfriend.

We all knew that most junior high relationships didn't last long, because I dated at least four boys in the eighth grade. The one thing that did not come up during that time was sex. I was not in that frame of mind and if the subject would have come up I really don't know how I would have reacted.

That was the year that I had my sex education class and with all that had happened to me, I really didn't know if I was prepared for that. After I was done with that class, everything seemed ok. I guess that I had pushed everything so far down inside of me that it didn't trigger any of those bad feelings. I just wanted to be normal and like the rest of my friends.

This year I also had my first experience with drugs. I was over to a friend's house sitting in the kitchen, when her brother came home and asked if we wanted to get high. I told him no and that I was scared because I had never done that before, and I wasn't sure if it would be ok to do that. We sat there for a while talking, eventually he convinced me to try it, so I did. Let me tell you if pigs could fly I think that I saw them. I was so out of my mind that all I could remember was saying to myself was that if I get back to my right mind that I would never touch drugs again.

Eventually, I came back to myself and I told both of them that I did not like the way that it made me feel and that was the last time that I would do that. I remember them saying to me that I blew my high because I was so paranoid. I was supposed to enjoy the feeling that it gave me. If that was supposed to be enjoyable, then just let me be miserable.

9.
DADDY

The summer before the ninth grade was one that I had the pleasure of meeting my father again. He was on vacation from the Army and was over to my grandmother's house in Grand Rapids, MI. He had gotten in touch with me through my uncle, Tommy, who is his bother.

Tommy had always kept in touch with me from time to time, even though my father didn't. My father had been married a couple of times and neither one of his wives wanted me to be apart of his life. So to take some of the heat off, my grandmother and uncles were there for me. I am not saying that my dad didn't love me, but he had another family to take care of.

I was so excited to see my dad and uncle drive up to my mother's house; they got out and spoke to everyone. Again just like he did when I was a two year old little girl, he told me to come and give him a hug. This time I had a choice in what I wanted to do, so I chose to turn down his request.

It had been 12 years since we had seen each other and I wasn't very happy about it either, plus I didn't know anything about him. I was very angry at him for not allowing me to be a part of his life, but I agreed to go with him back to my grandmother's house for a week.

When we got to my grandmother's house, there was a lady waiting for my dad, he introduced her to me as is new girlfriend Alice and that she would be spending time with us too. Well of course this made me even angrier with him, because I thought that he wanted to spend time alone with me, but I didn't say anything.

That was a very interesting week, because it started out with me being very angry at him and at the end of the week we become friends for the first time. This only happened because he had a lady in his life that cared enough the about both of us. She had taken the time out to talk to me about my dad; she began to tell me how much he loves me.

He had confided in her all the things that he had done over the years and that he just wanted a fresh start. Now I thought that if this lady (someone that I had just met) took the time to plead my dad's case, then maybe I could give him a chance.

The rest of the week was good, my dad and I sat down and talked about how we wanted our relationship to be, so from there we had no more problems. When it was time for him to take me back home, I wasn't ready to go, but I had to because it was getting close to time for school to start. We arrived back on a Friday afternoon. I kissed my dad goodbye and told him that I was sorry for the way that I acted in the beginning, and he promised me that I would always be apart of his life.

10.

EMERSON

The following Monday, I started helping my mother. She worked at the school during the summer because my stepfather gambled and she had to make sure that all of our bills were paid. A day or so before school started, she had asked me to go and get something from the car and on my way back I saw this girl going toward the library. I stopped her and introduced myself to her and asked her name. She told me that her name was Chan and that she had just moved here from Muskegon, with her mother and three of her siblings. They were living with her aunt down the street. We talked for a little longer and she told me that she would see me at school. During that year we became the best of friends, from getting into fights to sharing stories about good and bad relationships with our boyfriends, we went though it all together.

School started and that's when my real life as a teenager began. On the first day of school, I encountered, but a young lady that must have thought that she was the prettiest girl in school. Granted, she was very pretty, but much to her surprise there were a few of us who were just as pretty.

This young lady aggravated me on a daily basis, because she had several cousins there so if anything were to happen, they would defend her.

I worked in the lunchroom and she would always make little remarks toward me, but I would just ignore her. She would purposely bump into to me as we were changing classes', this went on for most of the year. One particular day, I was walking down the hall and this young lady approached me and spoke to me in a threatening voice regarding a young man. She told me that I had better leave him alone. I politely told her that I was not interested in him and that she had better not threaten me anymore about a boy. She continued to threaten me and I let her know that if I wanted him, that I would take him from her if she continued to harass me about him.

Now that might sound kind of cocky, but this young man had been trying to talk to me since the beginning of the school year and I did not want to have anything to do with him. I had gotten tired of her threats. The next day she continued to make little remarks and threats toward me, so guess what, later that day I saw him walking down the hall, we stopped and started talking and from that day on he was my boyfriend and any other boy that she was interested in.

What this girl didn't realize or even I didn't realize was that she was dealing with a real pro, it dawned on me that I was very manipulative and was not about to let this girl treat me like she did without a fight, not necessary a physical fight, but one that would show her who I was.

About midway through the school year, I had started to encounter more girls confronting me about all types of things. I was the type of person that didn't like confrontation or fighting. Some of the guys would come on very strong and some of the girls had a problem with that. I admit that I really enjoyed all of the attention that I was getting, so if that meant that I didn't make the situation any better, then I guess I didn't.

Later during the year, I was at my locker getting books for my next class when this same girl approached me again with some nonsense, repeating some "he say, she say" mess, not anything that I had said. When I tried to talk to her, she hit me and the only thing that I remember was someone trying to pull me off of her. I was taken to the waiting area by principal's office and my mother was called to come and get me. When she got there I was sitting there, very angry and wanting to tell my side of the story.

We went into the principal's office together and my mother explained to him what had been going on for the past few months. He explained to her that no matter what had happened that they had to kick me out for five days and that the other girl would only be kicked out for three days, because I wouldn't stop fighting when they told me to. I don't ever remember being so angry that I just wanted to hurt someone so bad, but that day I think that I had built up so much frustration from having to deal with the girls wanting to fight and me having to defend myself, that I just lost it.

After my mother and I left, I explained to her how I was feeling. She said that she understood because she had gone through a similar situation when she was growing up.

After I returned to school, everyone was treating me so different, no more getting picked on and the girls actually befriended me.

There was one boy in the ninth grade that I will probably never forget, his name was Pete; he was tall, dark and handsome. The way he wore his hair was very different from the other guys at school; it was short and curly. It was though most of the girls in school were talking about him because he was new to the school, and most of us wanted to be his girlfriend, and he chose me. He appeared to be much more mature than the other boys. He wanted to spend a lot of time together, at least until he wanted me to have sex with him and I wouldn't. Then he wanted to break up.

After Pete and I broke up, he started dating other girls at school. I started dating a high school guy named Keith. He was tall, dark, and very handsome. Every time I saw him, it made my heart melt. We made a lot of plans together; he was going to take me to my ninth grade prom among other things. At that time I was hanging out with Cynthia, I called her my big sister.

I spent a lot of time over her house helping her prepare for card parties that her mom had every weekend. This was so much fun for me; I helped Cynthia fry chicken wings and anything else that needed to be done. I honestly think that this was highlight of my weekend. Cynthia was a member of a singing group and they were preparing for an upcoming talent show, and they asked me to join.

One evening after rehearsal, we went back over to her house when I called Keith to let him know the good news, he was sounding really different; he told me that he didn't think that we should be dating anymore. We had been together for a couple of months and he was the first young man that I decided to have sex with.

This was a decision that took a while for me to make. A decision like that was a major one especially with my history. This was the first time that I had ever cried about breaking up with someone, he meant so much to me. I didn't know how I was going to get over him, even when I found out that he was also dating someone at the same school that he was attending. But with time, I got over it and I had to focus on something else.

Well it was time to start preparing for my freshman for the prom. I had no date because I was supposed to go with Keith, but we had broken up. I remembered that when I was in the sixth grade that I had made a promise to a friend. that no matter whom we were dating, we would go to the prom together. I called him and asked him did he remember the promise that we made to each other regarding the prom. He said, "yes," and he asked me again could be take me to my prom and I told him, "yes." We began to make big plans; we decided to wear yellow and black. We would have his sister and her boyfriend to escort us there and to dinner and we were going to have a good time.

Right before the prom, one of my closest friends betrayed me; I spent the night over her house. We had gotten really drunk. I had a crush on one of the guys at school. He was very popular and he also had a girlfriend. I had vowed never to tell him and I told my friend this in the deepest of confidence. I had gone so far as to carve his name in her floor with a knife. We made a promise to each other that no one would ever know about this crush.

When I got to school on Monday, I was confronted by his girlfriend wanting to fight. I had no idea what in the world she was talking about until she told me about the carving of his name in the floor, and then I knew that my friend had betrayed me. I was devastated because that information was very sacred and I trusted her to keep my secret. I explained to her the reasons and there was no way that I would even let him know. I remember saying to her who wouldn't like him, because he was so fine and very popular. After our conversation, she seemed to understand and we made everything alright between us and we actually became friends.

It was Prom Night and my date arrived to pick me up. Boy was he looking good! He was dressed in a black suit with a yellow shirt that matched my dress. This young man was so fine, he was medium built, and medium height and he had the smoothest dark caramel colored skin. He wore his hair in a medium length afro. We stayed at my house for a few minutes and took lots of pictures.

We entered the prom hand in hand, the music was nice and as we turned around to go to the dance floor, some of the other kids walked up to me and asked me did I know that my mother was there. I told them that I knew and that it didn't brother me at all because she had her own date. He was the Assistant Principal at my Junior High School and he had asked her to go because he had to chaperone, and that he needed a date. She looked so pretty and happy that night and I wasn't about to take that away from her.

My mother didn't seem to have any problem with me having a good time and vice versa. It was if neither one of us were there. After the prom we went to Wallis Supper Club for dinner and like the gentleman he always was, he escorted me home.

The remainder of the school year (which was about a week and a half to two weeks) was devoted to preparing for high school. About a week before school was out, I attended the boy's final track meet with some friends. There was a young man that I had seen earlier that year at a volleyball game. He was there with the same girl that I saw him with, and all I could do was look at him. So after the track meet I just spoke and left, but I vowed that he would be my boyfriend.

While I was leaving I was introduced to another young man named Elliott. He was very cute; he had a body to kill for and the sexiest lips. He talked so smooth that it would melt any girl's heart. He told me that he had just broken up with his girlfriend, and after a couple of days we started going together.

This was probably one of the worst boyfriends that I ever had; it was one of those love hate relationships. It was the end of the school year and I was really ready for the summer and all that was going to come along with it. I started hanging out with some of the girls at my church because I knew that they were friends with Elliott's ex-girlfriend and I wanted her to know that I was dating him now and I wanted her to leave him alone. But the joke was on me, because she let me know that they were still seeing each other. I would be over his house and she would come over, so instead of creating a problem I would just leave. There was no way that I was going to fight or even argue with her over him unless she hit me.

During the summer we continued to date, I was determined to get him from her. I would do almost anything to keep him even have sex with him. That didn't go to well because the kind of sex he wanted to have, I wasn't ready for. He made a few statements to me regarding the things that he and his ex could and would do. We were sitting in his family with his mom right in the kitchen while he was telling me this. After he was done talking, I politely got up and told him that he should go back with his ex, I got on my bike and went home.

The next day, I was standing in my front yard when I noticed two girls riding bikes coming toward me. It was Terry and one of her friends; she approached me stating that she was going to kick my butt, because she had told me that Elliott was her boyfriend and that I better leave him alone. If she would have stopped and listened to me for just a minute, she could have saved herself some stress, but she hit me and the fight began. After we were done fighting I told her that Elliott and I had broken up the day before, so her little ride was a waste of time and that she should go talk to him.

My mother was so mad that she called his mother, and told her what happened. His mother was also very angry with him for dating both of us. After they got off the phone, I got a call on my phone from Elliott apologizing to me for what happened and we decided to just be friends.

After our breakup, a couple of his friends thought that I would talk to them; one in particular, Joe. He started coming by my house unexpectedly. After about the third time I told him that there was no way that I would or could ever talk to one of my ex-boyfriend's friends and if he was a real friend he wouldn't have even try it, so I introduced him to my best friend and they began dating.

XI

NORTHWESTERN

It was the beginning of the new school year and I was in the 10th grade and I found out that Elliott was in my homeroom and the romance began again at least for a couple of weeks anyway. We would walk hand in hand to class; we'd try to see each other between classes and spend time together before going to he had to go to football practice. Everything was going good until I was informed that he was still involved with Terry.

Well that didn't go well with me, so I confronted him and he told me the truth. His reason was that she was having sex with him and I wasn't; I thought to myself, oh well and that's when the fight started. I hit him (I know it was wrong, but at the time I didn't care) with a book or something I really don't remember. He didn't hit me back, but he did hold my arms so that I couldn't hit him again.

We broke up for good that day, but I still cared a lot about him, so I would do stupid stuff to try and get his attention, but the only thing that it did was make him mad.

We were still in the same homeroom so I had to continue to see him first thing in the morning. I would stand in front of his locker and say things to him in class or simply talk to other guys in front of him to try and make him jealous. This went on for a couple of weeks until I got to the point that it just didn't even matter anymore, and so I didn't brother him or even speak to him for a while.

It was time for cheerleading try-outs and I let my cousin who was on the varsity cheerleading squad, talk me into trying out. I didn't make the squad because I didn't have a clue what I was doing, but they decided to let me be an extra. At the time I thought that was a good thing, but it really was an insult because they wanted me to be the team mascot. Someone quit and I ended up being a real cheerleader. I tried to make the best of it and I enjoyed it, but was a hard transition.

The school didn't allow us to travel to any of the games that were out of town, but that was ok with me.

We had a pretty good cheerleading squad; most of us became really good friends with the exception of one person. She wanted all the attention on her and the rest of us didn't matter to her. She treated us as if she thought she was better than the rest of us. We had created a challenging stunt and she want to be the one that was seen, so she volunteered to be the one to do it. This stunt called for her to be flipped upside down, but upon doing the flip she landed on her head and had to be rushed to the hospital. That evening was one of the hardest things that we had to feel. No matter how we felt about her we didn't want that to happen, but after that incident she was a totally different person and we all became even closer than before.

During basketball season, I met another young man, Mr. Popularity, Mr. Senior, Mr. Everything; at least that was what I called him. He was the most popular guy in the school. I was standing in the hall talking to one of my friends, when he walked up to me and started talking to me. I normally would have said something back, but he interrupted my conversation, so my friend and I walked away.

The next time that he saw me, he approached me like a gentleman. He asked me my name so I told him, and he told me his name. For the next couple of weeks he would walk me to all of my classes carrying my books and after school he walked me to cheerleading practice. What he didn't know was that my friends had already told me that it was a tradition that the senior guys would only talk to the sophomore girls to sleep with them and I of course was no exception.

Then one day we were walking to class and he asked me a crazy question, "would I get mad if he didn't call me?" My answer was no, I really didn't know a lot about him, because we only talked at school, and from that day forward we didn't talk any more. I didn't understand why at that time and I really didn't care. Later I found out that he wanted me to say yes so that would make him feel special.

After that short lived relationship there was really no else that I even wanted to talk to for a while until Mr. P. He wasn't the cutest guy at school, but he was very nice and he asked me to go to the Sadie Hawkins dance with him and I happily said yes. This was the first guy to let me drive; I hadn't taken driver's training and didn't know the first thing about it. He picked up me and my best friend and I begged him to let me drive, so he pulled over and let me behind the wheel. We only got about a half of a block when I hit something, he was scared that his mother was going to kill him that he immediately took me home, but he never told me what happened when is mother saw the car. That relationship didn't last very long, because we really did not have a lot in common, I guess not if someone wrecked your mother's car. His ex-girlfriend was getting very upset and I was interested in other guys, so after we went to the dance together we decided to just be friends.

As the year continued, I became good friends with a young lady named Glo. I had gone to Junior high school with Glo. We would call each other everyday, we met in the mornings before class, in between class and after school before leaving. We even knew when the other would be late for school. We became so close that we started hanging out together after school.

I still remained closed to my other friends especially my friend Leigh, she lived next door to a young lady that had a car, she would always let Leigh drive, so she would pick me up just to go riding. This particular day she called me and asked me to go riding, so we just rode around everywhere that we could think of to go. We were on our way to my house when we drove by Northwestern and there was a track meet going on, we decided to stop, and I am glad that we did.

As we entered the track meet we saw my "play" brother Rob, he attended Northern with my friend Leigh. We walked up the bleachers and sat down. I saw him, the guy that I had seen when I was in the ninth grade at the volleyball game and the track meet. This time he was talking with a different girl, so I asked Rob was that his girlfriend he told me that he didn't have a girlfriend that she was just a friend that he trained with, so I told him that I wanted to meet him.

Rob walked me up close to where he was sitting. When he saw me, he came down, sat next to me and introduced himself. His name was Ray and we continued to talk for the rest of the track meet. After it was over we walked down the stairs to go out the gate he asked me to wait for him, because he had to get all of his belongings from off the track. I asked Leigh if we could I wait for a few minutes so that I could talk to him.

When he came out of the gate he walked over to where were and started talking to us. He asked me for my phone number and you better know that I gave it to him. He walked me to the car and asked me if he could give me a goodbye kiss and I planted a kiss on him to remember. That kiss was so intense that I could hear everyone that was out there making noise. After we were done kissing, I got in the car with Leigh and he got into the car with Rob.

Later that night, I got a phone call from Ray just to tell me goodnight. The next day was the beginning of a new relationship. School was about to be out for the summer and I felt as though I was on top of the world. This was a guy that I wanted to meet for over a year and I finally got my chance.

This was a special summer for me, Ray was calling a lot and we got to know each other a lot better, we spent almost every waking moment on the phone and the rest of the time he would ride his bike or drive his brother's car over my house and stay until it was just about dark.

This was also the summer that I was turning 16. I was going to be able to get my Driver's License, so this was a big event for me, because my dad told me that he would buy me a new car. When it was time for me to take my Drivers Test, we ran into some problems my mother didn't have any insurance on her car so we had to call and get some on it, so I was able to take it. I was very nervous, because I had a problem with parallel parking, but I passed with flying colors.

Summer was over and I was in the Eleventh grade, it was very different, because Ray and I went to different schools. We knew that we were not going to see each other everyday like we did in the summer, but we didn't know how much it would bother us until it happened. So to compensate I didn't try out for the cheerleading squad so that we could spend more time together.

Ray's religion was a bit of a hindrance to our relationship, he was a Seventh Day Adventist which meant that he attended church on Saturday. We were just in high school and I enjoyed attending the school dances on Friday nights, Ray was not allowed to attend because of his religion. From sundown Friday night until sundown Saturday night, the only thing that they were allowed to do was listen to gospel music.

Glo and I continued to hang out together when I wasn't with Ray. We would still meet in the morning before class, between classes and after school before we left as we did the year before. Ray started talking to me about going to church with him, so I decided to go with him on a regular basis. I even became friends with three of his sisters. We even started doing a lot of things together. Ray had a twin sister named Fay, she was a very sweet young lady, but she was also a very quiet one too. She was a very good friend to me and I enjoyed her company a lot.

Ray and I had started having sex a few months into our relationship and that created a problem because we really had a lot of emotional ties to each other. We became very jealous of each other and then the distrust began, we would stay on the phone until all hours of the night just so neither one of us would call or talk to any one else. Now there was no reason for either one of us to do that, but it is funny how sex can change your whole attitude when it is done outside of marriage, it can totally play tricks on the mind.

We continued to date through out the year and our sexual activities became more intense. Ray would use is brother's car and we drive around to places that were quiet and have sex in the car. This happened so often that we lost control of the entire situation. Don't get me wrong I enjoyed everything about our relationship, but it was getting to be more than either one of us bargained for.   I think that I pulled him into something that he didn't have any control over.

Ray was addicted to me and I to him, we both were using sex to hold on to each other.   Later that year, things got a little shaky between us. Ray's mom thought that we were getting a little too close, which we probably were but I didn't want to hear that at the time.   He told me that she thought that we were too young to be so serious and I guess he agreed with her. He started seeing other girls and that made me angry but I would not say a lot about it, because I didn't want him to be angry with me. I loved him so much to the point that I would have done almost anything to keep him happy.

During the time this was going on, my best friend Chan was living with me. She had gotten so mad that she started introducing me to guys that she went to school with. Chan refused to let me be upset for long so we decided to start hanging out a lot more together. She convinced me to go to a talent show called the Beecher's Black Arts Festival. I agreed to go and my mother let me drive her new car. After the Black Arts Festival was over the traffic was very heavy and I had to hurry and get my mothers car back to her. So instead of waiting on the traffic to clear, I decided to drive over the grass and I ripped the muffler off the car. I was too scared to drive home because I thought that I would damage the car more and asked a friend to take me home.

When I got there I told my mother what happened, she started screaming at me telling me to go back and get her car. I walked back out the door, went back to the school and drove the car back home. I thought that she would never let me drive again; she just took the car to the shop to get it fixed and told me to me to be more careful when driving.

After that incident, I decided to ride with my friends for a while, because I felt so bad for damaging my mother's car. Ray and I were kind of broken up, but we continued to talk everyday. At that time I didn't understand that was his way of keeping me from going out with any other guys.

My friends were telling me that he had a girlfriend at the school that he attended but I didn't believe them, so I continued to talk to him. I continued to support him at the local track meets and tried to convince myself that everything was alright.

During the first part of the summer Ray and I got back together. Once again, we started having sex and using his brother's car. This continued to happen so much that I got pregnant, this devastated both of us. I wanted to have my baby, but Ray's family was so strict that he was terrified to even let them know. After talking about it for a little while, of course I gave in to what Ray wanted and that was to have an abortion.

I remember my mother saying to me that I should think carefully about becoming a mother, because there would be no way that I could take it back. I told her that I didn't want to have a baby right now and she could call the doctor's office to schedule me an appointment to have an abortion.

After I came home from the hospital, Ray was there, he laid down beside me and apologized with tears in his eyes. He confessed to me that he didn't want me to do that, but he didn't know what else to do and that he didn't ever want to have another child after giving this one up. After that, Ray became very protective of me; well at least for a little while.

I was back to my old self again and I was planning to take my senior pictures and Ray wanted to be a part of that. He asked me could he take pictures with me and I said yes. I had so much fun taking my pictures because I was so excited to be a High School Senior. After I was finished taking my pictures, Ray and I dated for a few more weeks and then broke up again.

That summer I did a lot; from getting my first hooptie to finally having the courage to go out with other boys. My best friend Chan and I partied until we couldn't party anymore. Chan was raised totally different than I was; she was the babysitter for her younger brothers and sister. Her mother really didn't allow her to do the things that I was allowed to do. She had just ended a relationship with her boyfriend and was a little unhappy about it, so I spent the night over her house.

Her mother worked third shift, which left us there alone, I told her that I wanted to go to the party across the street at the clubhouse where she lived. At the time I liked a guy that she attended school with and he was going to be at the party. Chan was very skeptical about going, because she knew that if her mother found out, that we would be in big trouble.

Of course, we went to the party anyway. Chan was scared out of her mind and I didn't have a care in the world; I was the daredevil. I met up with Wayne and we talked and kissed most of the night, and I had no idea where Chan was for a little while, but eventually I caught up with her and told her that I was leaving with Wayne because I wanted to go for a ride.

She starting screaming at me not to go and saying to me, what if my mama comes home before you get back, and I told her that I would not be long. I left with Wayne. We just rode around for a while and then we stopped and parked. He asked me to sit on his lap and we begin kissing again until we couldn't kiss anymore.

I think that we were gone about two hours and I remember that I had to get back before Chan's mother got home. I told him that I had to go and he took me back.   After that night I didn't see Wayne again, because he told me that he wanted to have sex with me that night and if I couldn't do that, he would find someone that wanted to.

Of course it hurt, but what else could I do at that moment.   By the next party I had met another guy, Eric, and we began talking, we would meet at parties and then we would leave and go over to his house. Eric was the one that I thought could help me get over Ray, so I slept with him throughout the summer.   After a while it got old and neither of us wanted it anymore, and so we decided to go our separate ways, but continued a great friendship.

Most of my friends were at Beecher and I asked my mother about attending Beecher my last year. At first she was going to let me and I think that I did something stupid to make her very angry and she changed here mind. I cried thinking that it would change her mind, but it didn't and I ended right back at the same school.

It was my senior year in High School. Glo and I were a team again, back to our old routine. Ray and I got back together over the summer only because he was scared that he was loosing me. But that didn't last long; as soon as he thought that I was not talking to other guys anymore he was up to his old tricks.

About a week after school, started there was this young man walking down the hall; he was about six feet tall, his complexion was medium brown and he was so handsome. His name was Larry, he was very quiet, he played football and basketball and he seemed to be very intelligent and mannerable. We began to talk for a while, but of course Ray found out and cried to get me back. This time he promised that he would not cheat on me again, I listened to him and lost Larry.

The rest of the school year I concentrated on the National Honor Society's plans, getting scholarships to attend Michigan State and my Senior Prom and the prom committee. I had joined the Seventh Day Adventist religion and I could not attend the prom if it was on a Friday night. So we worked very hard to get it on a Saturday night. That process became harder and harder, because most of the places that we tried to get had already been booked.

This was very disappointing to me, because I was about to miss my senior prom. Then about a month or two later, Joe came to my classroom with some good news, he told me that he had found a place that was available on a Saturday. When school got out that day I called Ray and told him the good news, he seemed very excited and we began to make plans to attend. I shopped continuously for a prom dress and I couldn't find what I wanted so I decided to get one made. Ray and I came to an agreement to wear pink and black.

During the time that I was preparing for my prom, I got a phone call from my best friend regarding a mutual friend (my cousin). She was dating Ray. I called her up (something I wouldn't normally do), but she was someone that I had confided in about my relationship with Ray. We talked on the phone almost every day and I guess she forgot to tell me that they had been seeing each other. I asked her about it and she started crying and saying that she was sorry.

She told me that he had asked her to go to the prom with him and I politely told her that he wouldn't be going to the prom with anyone but me. She also told me that she had heard that he had also asked another young lady to the prom. I again reminded her of what I had said earlier; I really didn't care who he had asked or what he had done. Later I found out that they had been seeing each other for quite some time, I again called her and told her that our friendship was over.

It was the night I had been waiting for, Prom Night. Ray picked me up in his brother's 1978 black thunderbird it was so sharp. We took lots of pictures and then we left to go to the prom, which was held at the Grand Blanc Country Club. When we got there, there were so many people out there just looking as each couple arrived; this made me feel like a celebrity. We went in to our assigned seats, danced for a while, took pictures and left. We went to dinner and after dinner we went back to my house. Ray stayed for a couple of hours and than went home. Most of the couples had made plans to go to Cedar Point after the prom, but Ray's parents would not allow him to go since it was an overnight trip.

After all the excitement of the prom, I started getting ready for my honors assembly. I was so happy, because I had been accepted at Michigan State University. I also had received several scholarships, one full academic scholarships and some small scholarship that I had applied for.

12.

GRADUATION

We received our Cap and Gowns about two weeks before graduation and strutted around the city like we owned it. School ended for the seniors about a week before graduation.

The morning of our ceremony we had to meet at the IMA for rehearsal, we were lined up in alphabetical order and we were required to walk across the stage and go down and be seated in order. After rehearsal, I went home to get ready for the real thing. I called Ray to ask him if would he be attending my graduation as planned and he assured me that he would be there. I had to be at the IMA at 5:00pm, because the ceremony started at 7:00pm so that we could all be lined up and ready to start on time. I remember being very nervous, but very proud about my accomplishment.

My mother got there about 6:00pm and took lots of pictures, as I turned around to talk to some friends I saw my uncles and my grandmother from Grand Rapids, I hadn't seen them in a while, but I very glad to see them.

It was time to march in and be seated, Row by row and one by one they called us up to the stage. It was my turn to receive my paper and all I remember was being so excited that I almost fell. After the ceremony I was asked to go out with my friends, but I decided to go home and visit with Ray, but when I talked to him he that said he couldn't come over that night. So I stayed home with my family and listened to music and talked to them.

I had officially graduated and I had some hard decisions to make, I really loved Ray and he was also going away to school, we didn't want to lose contact with each other, so me being the person that I was, I decided to forfeit my scholarships and stay home and go to a local college.

Ray and I continued dating during the summer and even when he left for college. That summer was life changing for me . . . changing from a girl to a woman.

This is the beginning stages of a caterpillar, the
egg to the larva. . . . .

Commentaries

Upon reading *From a Caterpillar to a Butterfly,* you will find yourself living through the experience. Author Renetta Randle vividly captures your heart as she describes in raw detail the incestuous atrocities that no child should be subjected to. You must be ready for reality before opening these pages. I've known her for three years, and it was not possible to know that she had suffered such cruelty. She communicates in a superbly wonderful, above-board manner; and pours her heart and soul into everyone and everything she commits to. If you happen to be her friend – and I am – you are blessed. It is refreshing and exciting to be associated with someone who has the courage to share the deepest and darkest secrets of her life with the world, and has transformed these challenges into victories.

Fern Rayon-Wilson, Graphic Designer

I have known Renetta Randle for approximately 20 years. I have seen her transform from a caterpillar to a butterfly. I have counseled victims of incest for almost 30 years and I know the struggle involved in the process. It is very difficult for children and adults to talk about this issue. It is an issue that is often difficult for society to talk about. When Renetta talked about writing about her experience, I asked her was she sure she wanted the world to know about her experience. She told me that she was willing to do whatever it takes to help other victims of sexual abuse. She was so excited about writing this book in order to help other people talk about this issue. It was exciting for me to watch her emerge from a caterpillar to a butterfly. I am so proud of her, and all of the time, energy and excitement that she put in to developing this book. I am pleased to introduce to you, my friend, confidante, writer and minister of healing past hurts-Renetta Randle.

Sheryl Y. Strothers, ACSW,BCD, Mental Health Therapist

It is by no accident you're reading this book today!

TO ORDER COPIES OF OTHER BOOKS THROUGH
SHORTCAKES PRODUCTIONS
PLEASE FILL OUT THE FORM BELOW

☐   ☐   **CHECK   MONEY ORDER**

Signature_____

Name_____

Address_____

City_____State_____Zip_____

Phone_____E-Mail_____

Check the books that you'd like to order on the line below:

QTY

___From A Caterpillar To A Butterfly $16.00

___Other_____

_____

Make all checks or money orders payable to Shortcake's Productions
(Add .06 cent sales tax on the dollar + $2 for S&H)
Example: $19.96+($1.14 for sales tax)+($2.00 S&H)= $23.10
Use the back of form for additional inquiries.
Thanks for your support
Clip and mail completed form to:

Shortcake's Productions   810.394.4467
An Affiliate of Flo's Productions
Website: www.shortcakesproductions.com